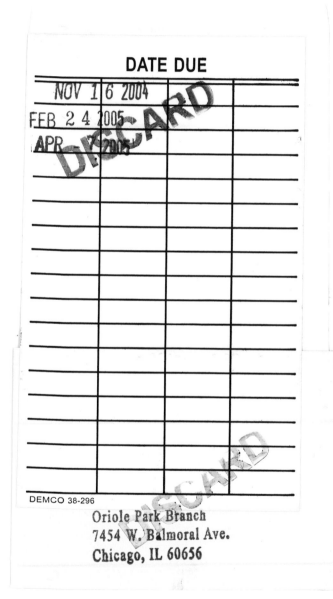

The Amazing Book of
MAMMAL RECORDS

The Largest, the Smallest, the Fastest, and Many More!

By Samuel G. Woods

Illustrations by Jeff Cline

BLACKBIRCH PRESS, INC.

WOODBRIDGE, CONNECTICUT

For Nathan and Emma, my two favorite mammals.
–SGW

Published by Blackbirch Press, Inc.
260 Amity Road
Woodbridge, CT 06525
web site: http://www.blackbirch.com
e-mail: staff@blackbirch.com

© 2000 Blackbirch Press, Inc.
First Edition

Printed in China

10 9 8 7 6 5 4 3 2 1

Photo Credits
Cover: ©PhotoDisc; title page and table of contents: ©PhotoDisc; page 5: ©Mike Johnson/Innerspace Visions; page 7: ©Merlin Tuttle/Photo Researchers; pages 8, 10-12, 14, 16, 20, 24, 26, 28, 29: ©Corel Corporation; pages 13, 15, 17-19, 21-23, 25, 27, 30: ©PhotoDisc; page 9: ©Digital Stock.

Library of Congress Cataloging-in-Publication Data
Woods, Samuel G.
    The amazing book of mammal records: the largest, the smallest, the fastest, and many more! / by Samuel G. Woods; illustrations by Jeff Cline.
        p.   cm.
    Includes bibliographical references (p.) and index.
    Summary: Introduces, in question and answer format, such record-breaking mammals as the cheetah, blue whale, koala, giraffe, and water buffalo.
        ISBN 1-56711-367-2
    1. Mammals—Miscellanea—Juvenile literature. [1. Mammals—Miscellanea. 2. Questions and answers.] I. Cline, Jeff, ill. II. Title
QL706.2.W65   2000   99–042523
599—dc21   CIP

Contents

What's the LARGEST Mammal?

The Blue Whale

Blue whales are the largest animals on the planet. An average blue whale grows to a length of 100 feet (30.5 m) and can weigh up to 260,000 pounds (117,940 kg). That's about the weight of 10 school buses! (A blue whale's heart alone can weigh about 2,000 pounds [907 kg], that's the weight of a small car!)

NOTEPAD

The world's largest animals eat some of the world's smallest animals, called krill (tiny shrimp-like crustaceans). A blue whale can eat up to 8,000 pounds (3,600 kg) of krill in one day! Blue whales also have the world's largest babies. Newborns can weigh 16,000 pounds (7,257 kg) and be 23 feet (7 m) long. They can drink up to 160 gallons (600 liters) of milk per day!

NOTEWORTHY: Blue whales are endangered. There are only an estimated 350 alive today.

What's the SMALLEST Mammal?

The Kitti's Hog-Nosed Bat

This teeny tiny mammal averages only about 1 inch (3 cm) in length and weighs only about as much as a dime. Full-grown, its body is no bigger than a bumblebee!

Kitti's hog-nosed bats are microbats, which are the smallest kind of bats.

What's the FASTEST Mammal?

The Cheetah

The fastest cheetahs have been clocked running more than 70 miles (113 km) per hour. What's more, they can maintain their high speed for about 500 yards (457 m) at a time. Like a fine sports car, a cheetah can go from 0 to 60 mph (97 kph) in about 3 seconds!

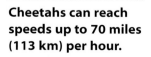

Cheetahs can reach speeds up to 70 miles (113 km) per hour.

NOTEPAD

Cheetahs are excellent hunters. Unlike other cats, they chase down prey instead of ambushing and pouncing. Their sharp claws do not retract (move in and out) the way other cats' claws do. Sadly, cheetahs have been hunted to near extinction by humans. Today, they are found only in parts of southern Africa.

What's the SLOWEST Mammal?

SLOTH RACES

The Three-Toed Sloth

On land, the average sloth will crawl along at about .07 miles (.11 km) per hour. At that rate, it would take nearly 15 hours to travel 1 mile (1.6 km)!

NOTEPAD

Three-toed sloths are found mostly in the rain forests of South America. High up in trees, they spend their lives hanging upside down. They eat, sleep, and even give birth upside down! They move so little, and so slowly, that algae actually grows on their fur! In a green rain forest, this camouflages them well.

What's the LAZIEST Mammal?

❖ ❖ ❖ ❖ ❖ ❖ ❖

The Koala

A koala sleeps about 22 hours out of every day!

NOTEPAD

Koalas are marsupials (pouched mammals) that are found only in Australia. While awake, they eat between 1–2 pounds (520–1,000 g) of eucalyptus leaves each day. But they are picky. They will only eat 12 of the 100 varieties of eucalyptus. Koalas never drink. They get all the moisture they need from their food.

What's the LARGEST Carnivore (Meat-Eater)?

The Polar Bear

A full-grown polar bear can weigh up to 1,300 pounds (589 kg) and can stand up to 11 feet (3.3 m) tall! An average polar bear foot is about 12 inches (30 cm) long and 10 inches (25 cm) wide.

A full-grown polar bear can weigh up to 1,300 pounds (589 kg).

NOTEPAD

The Earth's largest carnivores have big appetites. They use a great deal of energy while swimming, which they do extremely well. Some polar bears have been seen swimming 50 miles (32 km) between ice and shore. Their main food is seals. A single polar bear will often eat an entire seal.

NOTEWORTHY: Polar bear populations have been decreasing rapidly in recent years. There are only an estimated 40,000 bears left in the wild.

What's the TALLEST Mammal?

SAY AHHHHH...

Giraffe necks have special blood vessels in them that control blood flow.

The Giraffe

Most full-grown giraffes stand about 17 feet (5 m) high. A giraffe's tongue alone can be about 18 inches (45 cm) long!

NOTEPAD

A giraffe's neck contains the same number of bones (vertebrae) as a human neck. But each of a giraffe's vertebrae is greatly elongated. Giraffes have very elastic blood vessels in their necks that control blood flow. This is important when a giraffe bends over to drink or tend its young. If all the blood from the neck rushed to its head at once, it would pass out!

What's the BIGGEST Primate?

The Gorilla

Full-grown male gorillas weigh up to 600 pounds (272 kg) and can stand more than 6 feet (1.8 m) tall!

Gorillas are vegetarians that eat mostly fruit, leaves, and stems.

NOTEPAD

Primate is the mammal order to which humans belong. Like humans, gorillas are highly intelligent and social creatures. Social grooming, which gorillas do affectionately with one another, relaxes them and bonds them. Unlike most humans, gorillas are entirely vegetarian. They mainly eat fruit, leaves, and juicy stems of plants. Most gorillas can live to be somewhere between 30 and 40 years of age.

What's the Mammal That TRAVELS FARTHEST?

The Northern Elephant Seal

These large seals travel an average of 12,000 to 13,000 miles (19,000 to 21,000 km) each year. Most can swim about 60 miles (96 km) per day!

Elephant seals warm themselves on the shore in the sun. Inset: a male (bull).

NOTEPAD

Elephant seals make their long journeys twice a year, once after mating and once after molting (shedding their fur and an outer layer of skin). Most will travel between the southernmost tip of California to the northern waters of Alaska. Elephant seals are amazing divers. Many can dive down more than 5,100 feet (1,560 m) and can stay under water up to 11 hours at a time!

What's the LARGEST Land Mammal?

The African Elephant

A full-grown male African elephant can weigh up to 13.5 tons (12.3 metric tons). That's the weight of about 7 sport-utility vehicles!

A full-grown elephant can eat up to 500 pounds (227 kg) of food in a day.

NOTEPAD

The Earth's largest land mammal stands about 10 feet (3 m) high from toe to shoulder. This vegetarian can eat up to 500 pounds (227 kg) of food each day and can drink up to 40 gallons (151 l) of water at one time! An elephant only has about 6 teeth, which it uses to grind food. At about age 70, it will lose its teeth, stop eating, and will die of starvation.

NOTEWORTHY: African elephants are endangered. Only an estimated 100,000 are alive today.

Which Mammal Builds the LARGEST HOME?

The Black-tailed Prairie Dog

Prairie dogs have been known to build underground burrows that can house up to 400 million animals! One burrow in Texas was estimated to be about 250 miles (402 km) long and 100 miles (160 km) wide!

Prairie dog towns are so well built that many will last for hundreds of years.

What's the Mammal With the LONGEST HORNS?

The Water Buffalo

A water buffalo's horns can grow as long as 13 feet (4 m). That's longer than two adult men lined up end to end!

NOTEPAD

These large marsh-dwelling mammals may look harmless, but they can be quite dangerous if alarmed. Some adult males can weigh roughly 4,000 pounds (1,800 kg) and can stand 6 feet (2 m) high from foot to shoulder. Their size and weight, combined with long, sharp horns, make them a difficult and challenging target, even for a group of hungry lions.

Large size and long, sharp horns make water buffalo potentially dangerous.

What's the LARGEST Rodent?

Capybaras are found only in South America.

The Capybara

These hairy, pig-like animals can weigh up to 175 pounds (79 kg) and can grow to nearly 5 feet (1.5 m) long.

NOTEPAD

Capybaras are found on the swampy grasslands of South America. They live in small herds of up to 20 animals and spend a good deal of time in or near the water. They have webbed feet and are excellent swimmers. Like all rodents, a capybara's teeth are continously growing—they replenish themselves as they are worn down by gnawing on tough plants and grasses.

What's the LONGEST-LIVED Mammal?

The Killer Whale

The average lifespan of a killer whale is 90 years (the average for humans is only a bit more than 76 years).

Killer whales are the largest members of the dolphin family.

Killer whales are also known as orcas. They are the largest members of the dolphin family. Orcas are some of the fastest-swimming marine mammals, able to reach speeds of 30 miles (48 k) per hour. Killer whales are found mostly in the colder waters of the North and South poles. Because each whale has a uniquely shaped dorsal (top) fin, scientists can identify and track individuals for study.

Glossary

Algae—small plants without roots or stems that grow on water or other damp surfaces.

Ambush—to hide and then attack.

Camouflage—blending in well with the surroundings.

Carnivore—a meat-eater.

Echolocation—a way for certain animals to find objects by sending out sound waves and seeing how long they take to bounce back. The longer it takes for the waves to bounce back, the farther away the object.

Endangered species—a plant or animal that is in danger of becoming extinct.

Marsupial—the name for a group of animals in which the females carry their young in pouches on their abdomens.

Molting—when an animal or bird sheds its outer layer of fur, skin, or feathers so that a new layer can grow in.

Prey—an animal that is hunted by another for food.

Retract—to pull or move backward.

Sound wave—a series of vibrations that can be heard in air, solids, or liquids.

For More Information

Books

Hare, Dr. Tony. Alison Warner. *Animal Fact-File: Head-to-Tail Profiles of over 90 Mammals.* New York, NY: Facts on File, Inc., 1999.

Peissel, Michel. Allen, Missy (Contributor). *Dangerous Mammals* (Encyclopedia of Danger). New York, NY: Chelsea House, 1993.

Stotsky, Sandra. *Amazing Mammals* (Ranger Rick's Naturescope). New York, NY: Chelsea House, 1999.

Video

Hartley, Mariette. Brion James. *The Amazing World of Marine Mammals* (1997).

Web Sites

Marsupial Mammals

Facts and photographs about marsupials and their habitat—
www.ucmp.berkeley.edu/mammal/marsupial/marsupial.html

Sea World Animal Bytes

Find out exciting information about many different mammals—
www.seaworld.org/animal_bytes/animal_bytes.html

Index